The
Third Angel's
Message
and the
Book of Joel

The Day Is at Hand

Joseph Farah

AB ASPECT Books
www.ASPECTBooks.com

Copyright © 2014 Joseph Farah
Copyright © 2014 ASPECT Books
ISBN-13: 978-1-4796-0367-1 (Paperback)
ISBN-13: 978-1-4796-0368-8 (ePub)
ISBN-13: 978-1-4796-0369-5 (Kindle / Mobi)

All scripture quotations are taken from the King James Version Bible. Public domain.

Published by

AB **ASPECT Books**
www.ASPECTBooks.com

Table of Contents

Introduction

Throughout the Bible different authors of scripture foretold when the great day of the Lord would be near at hand. Jesus himself said, "So likewise ye, when ye shall see all these things, know that it is near, even at the doors. Verily I say unto you, This generation shall not pass, till all these things be fulfilled" (Matt. 24:33, 34). Through a study of prophecy, it may be known when we have come to the generation that will not pass before Christ returns in the clouds of glory.

The Word of God has not left us ignorant regarding such a momentous event. "Surely the Lord GOD will do nothing, but he revealeth his secret unto his servants the prophets" (Amos 3:7). Although no one knows the day or the hour of His return, we may discern the signs of the times (Matt. 16:3). Of that day, Ellen White wrote, "Though no man knoweth the day nor the hour of His coming, we are instructed and required to know when it is near. We are further taught that to disregard His warning, and refuse or neglect to know when His advent is near, will be as fatal for us as it was for those who lived in the days of Noah not to know when the flood was coming" (*The Great Controversy*, p. 371).

The apostle Paul wrote something similar in nature, "But ye, brethren, are not in darkness, that that day should overtake you as a thief. Ye are all the children of light, and the children of the day: we are not of the night, nor of darkness" (1 Thess. 5:4, 5). We have been instructed that "we have also a more sure word of prophecy; whereunto ye do well that ye take heed, as unto a light that shineth in a dark place, until the day dawn, and the day star arise in your hearts" (2 Peter 1:19). The dawning of that day refers to the second coming of Christ in power and glory. Enough has been revealed in God's word that we may know when the day of the Lord is near and when we have come to the last generation that will be alive at Christ's second coming. "For the secret things belong unto the LORD our God: but those things which are revealed belong unto us and to our children for ever" (Deut. 29:29).

The pioneers of the Adventist Church believed that through a study of God's Word we may anticipate the approach of Christ's kingdom and know the generation which is to witness its establishment (Smith, *Daniel and the Revelation*, p. 65). Ellen White wrote that the believer "has a chart pointing out every waymark on the heavenward journey, and he ought not to guess at anything" (*The Great Controversy,* p. 598). The fulfillment of prophetic events has been recorded on the pages of history, and we may be confident that "all which is yet to come will be fulfilled in its order" (*Prophets and Kings,* p. 536). The books of Joel, Luke, James, and Zephaniah have given us prophetic signs that we may know when Jesus' coming is near at hand.

The special focus of this booklet will be on the third angel's message and its relation to the book of Joel. The year 2008 was a prophetically significant year informing us that Jesus is at the door and that this present "generation shall not pass away, till all be fulfilled" (Luke 21:32). The prophets have spoken more for our present day and for the generations that have followed them than for the times in which they lived (White, "Heart Piety Essential," *The Signs of the Times,* April 2, 1896). We have been instructed that "all these things happened unto them for ensamples: and they are written for our admonition, upon whom the ends of the world are come" (1 Cor. 10:11).

The Great Disappointment

In Revelation 10 we read of a mighty angel coming down from heaven. He is clothed with a cloud, and a rainbow is upon His head. His face resembles the sun and His feet are as pillars of fire. This mighty angel who talked with John was Jesus Christ (White, *Christ Triumphant,* p. 344). He has in His hand an open book, which is the prophetic book of Daniel (White, *Manuscript Releases,* vol. 19, p. 320). When He cried with a loud voice, seven thunders uttered their voices. The seven thunders were an outline of events that were to transpire under the first and second angel's messages (White, *Manuscript Releases,* vol. 1, p. 99).

The posture of the mighty angel, with His right foot upon the sea and His left foot on the earth, indicates that this message was to be a worldwide proclamation (Rev. 10:2). The Advent movement was not restricted to the Northeast of America or to the Millerites. William Miller said, "One or two in every quarter of the globe have proclaimed the news, and all agree in the time"

(Loughborough, *The Great Second Advent Movement,* p. 105). The advent message was proclaimed in the years 1840 to 1844 and culminated in the midnight cry that commenced in the summer of 1844. When the expected time for Jesus' return passed, the Advent believers experienced a great disappointment, which was prophesied about in Revelation 10:

And I went unto the angel, and said unto him, Give me the little book. And he said unto me, Take it, and eat it up; and it shall make thy belly bitter, but it shall be in thy mouth sweet as honey. And I took the little book out of the angel's hand, and ate it up; and it was in my mouth sweet as honey: and as soon as I had eaten it, my belly was bitter (Rev. 10:9, 10).

Although they were mistaken in their belief that Jesus would return in 1844, they were nonetheless led by the Spirit of God. Their calculation of the time prophecy in Daniel 8:14 was correct, but they were mistaken as to the nature of the event to take place. The angel informs John that the believers "must prophesy again before

It wasn't until four years after the Great Disappointment that the clear light of the third angel was revealed and the proclamation of the message began.

9

many peoples, and nations, and tongues, and kings" (Rev. 10:11). They had to go back and study the Bible, including the sanctuary message and proclaim the third angel's message. Up to the time of October 22, 1844, the third angel's message was not being proclaimed. It wasn't until four years after the Great Disappointment that the clear light of the third angel was revealed and the proclamation of the message began.

The Third Angel's Message

As Jesus moved from the Holy Place into the Most Holy Place, He sent another angel with a third message to the world. Ellen White wrote, "As the ministration of Jesus closed in the holy place, and He passed into the holiest, and stood before the ark containing the law of God, He sent another mighty angel with a third message to the world" (*Early Writings,* p. 254).

Although the message of the third angel was sent in 1844, it was not completely understood by the Advent believers. The period from 1844 until the third angel's message was understood was a perplexing time for them (Loughborough, *The Great Second Advent Movement,* p. 235). The truth emanating from the third angel was

In 1847, Elder Himes said, "The fourteenth chapter [of Revelation] presents an astounding cry [of the third angel's message], yet to be made, as a warning to mankind."

likened to the rays of the sun coming over the horizon during the early dawn; however, its brilliant core was not yet seen. In 1847, Elder Himes said, "The fourteenth chapter [of Revelation] presents an astounding cry [of the third angel's message], yet to be made, as a warning to mankind" (Ibid., p. 247).

In order for the Advent believers to fully understand the third angel's message, two important truths had to be brought to light: the Sabbath and the "sealing message." The third angel's message is based on the idea that the

> *In order for the Advent believers to fully understand the third angel's message, two important truths had to be brought to light: the Sabbath and the "sealing message."*

Sabbath is the seal of God. At the time of the Great Disappointment in 1844, God in His providence provided certain verses in scripture to direct the attention of the believers to the heavenly sanctuary and to the Decalogue, particularly the Sabbath commandment. Revelation 14:12 reads, "Here is the patience of the saints: here are they that keep the commandments of God, and the faith of Jesus." The Advent believers needed considerable patience during their great disappointment. The latter part of the verse captures the attention of the believer to contemplate the Ten Commandments as given by God.

The Great Disappointment is prophesied about in Revelation 10:9–11. The verse after that reads, "And there was given me a reed like unto a rod: and the angel stood, saying, Rise, and measure the temple of God, and the altar, and them that worship therein" (Rev. 11:1). At the time John wrote these words, the temple in Jerusalem lay in ruins. It is no doubt that John was directing the reader to "measure" the heavenly sanctuary. The apostle was encouraging the believers to carefully study what events were transpiring in the Holy Place and Most Holy Place starting in 1844.

The prophecy of Daniel 8:14 directs the attention of the reader to the cleansing of the heavenly sanctuary, which was to take place after the 2,300 day time period: "And he said unto me, Unto two thousand and three hundred days; then shall the sanctuary be cleansed." As believers follow Jesus into the Most Holy Place by faith, their attention is directed to the ark of the covenant which contains the Decalogue with the Sabbath commandment at its center.

The Sabbath Truth and the Sealing Message

One of the pioneers who first accepted the Sabbath truth was Joseph Bates. Elder Bates accepted the Sabbath in 1845 (Loughborough, *The Great Second Advent Movement: Its Rise and Progress,* p. 250). In 1846 Ellen White had a vision of the Most Holy Place, the ark of the covenant, and the tables of stone with a halo around the fourth commandment (White, *Early Writings*, p. 33). She saw that the Sabbath commandment was not nailed to the cross. God did not change the Sabbath; instead, the pope had substituted the first day of the week for the seventh day of the week as specified in the fourth commandment. In 1847 Ellen White received light concerning the mark of the beast.

> *In 1846 Ellen White had a vision of the Most Holy Place, the ark of the covenant, and the tables of stone with a halo around the fourth commandment.*

I saw all that "would not receive the mark of the Beast, and of his Image, in their foreheads or in their hands," could not buy or sell. I saw that the number (666) of the Image Beast was made up; and that it was the Beast that changed the Sabbath, and the Image Beast had followed on after, and kept the Pope's, and not God's Sabbath. And all we were required to do, was to give up God's Sabbath, and keep the Pope's, and then we should have the mark of the Beast, and of his image. (*A Word to the Little Flock*, p. 19)

In the following year, 1848, a total of seven Sabbath conferences were held. During this time the Advent believers studied Scripture, and the Holy Spirit unfolded great truths. The pillars of the church were established. At the seventh conference, Ellen White had a vision regarding the "sealing truth." She said, "At a meeting held in Dorchester, Mass., November, 1848, I had been given a view of the proclamation of the sealing message, and of the duty of the brethren to publish the light that was shining upon our pathway" (*Life Sketches of Ellen G. White*, p. 125). Elder James White, in giving his account of this meeting wrote that Sister White described the Sabbath light as the sealing truth (Ibid., p. 116). We have further been instructed that the seal of the living God is contained in the third angel's message (*Manuscript Releases*, vol. 13, p. 268).

The year 1848 was a special time in Adventist history. The truths of the third angel's message were established and the way opened for the advancement of the work (Loughborough, *The Great Second Advent Movement: Its Rise and Progress*, p. 270). During the Sabbath conferences, the work of uniting the believers on the great truths connected with the third angel's message commenced (Emmerson, *The Reformation and the Advent Movement,* p. 206). The third angel's message rose to its height and its broad, distinct disc was clear as the noonday sun that year (Loughborough, *The Great Second Advent Movement: Its Rise and Progress*, p. 464).

> *The year 1848 was a special time in Adventist history. The truths of the third angel's message were established and the way opened for the advancement of the work*

The Third Angel's Message and the Spirit of Prophecy

The third angel's message is given special attention in the writings of Ellen White. She declared that it is "the theme of greatest importance ... embracing the messages of the first and second angels" (*Evangelism,* p. 196). It is also the "Gospel message for these last days" (*The Kress Collection*, p. 102). Mrs. White said, "The present truth for this time comprises the messages, the third angel's message succeeding the first and the second" (*Manuscript Releases*, vol. 9, p. 291).

J. N. Loughborough states that the third angel's message was the precursor to the Great Second Advent Movement (*The Great Second Advent Movement: Its Rise and Progress*, p. vii). He calls it the most solemn warning in the entire Bible, a denunciation of wrath so dreadful to which no threat can compare (Ibid., p. 247). Ellen White wrote that it's a "fearful warning, with the most terrible threatening ever borne to man" (*Early Writings*, p. 254).

The Third Angel's Message and the Book of Joel

The third angel's message reads:

> And the third angel followed them, saying with a loud voice, If any man worship the beast and his image, and receive his mark in his forehead, or in his hand, the same shall drink of the wine of the wrath of God, which is poured out without mixture into the cup of his indignation; and he shall be tormented with fire and brimstone in the presence of the holy angels, and in the presence of the Lamb: And the smoke of their torment ascendeth up for ever and ever: and they have no rest day nor night, who worship the beast and his image, and whosoever receiveth the mark of his name. Here is the patience of the saints: here are they that keep the commandments of God, and the faith of Jesus. (Rev. 14:9–12)

When Scripture says, "the same shall drink of the wine of the wrath of God, which is poured out without mixture," we understand that to mean the unmingled wrath of God without mercy. The mark of the beast represents Sunday observance; however, this is not the case at this present time. When Sunday observance is enforced by law, those who choose to obey a human precept despite the clear light of the true Sabbath will receive the mark of the beast (*Evangelism*, p. 233). The question we now ask is, how will this wrath be "poured out" or manifested?

The following verses reveal that the wrath of God is contained in the seven last plagues. "And I saw another sign in heaven, great and marvellous, seven angels having the seven last plagues; for in them is filled up the wrath of God" (Rev. 15:1). "And one of the four beasts gave unto the seven angels seven golden vials full of the wrath of God, who liveth for ever and ever" (Rev. 15:7). This great manifestation of God's wrath and the reaction of the unrighteous is described in Revelation 6:16, 17: "And said to the mountains and rocks, Fall on us, and hide us from the face of him that sitteth on the throne, and from the wrath of the Lamb: For the great day of his wrath is come; and who shall be able to stand?"

> *The message we bear to the world has the seal of the living God.*

The phrase "the great day of His wrath" is a New Testament reference to the "great day of the Lord," which the prophet Zephaniah described as a day of wrath

19

(Zeph. 1:14, 15). We can deduct that the third angel's message is a warning against the day of the Lord. Consider the following quotes from the Spirit of Prophecy:

> Who are proclaiming the message of the third angel, calling the world to make ready for the great day of God? (*Testimonies for the Church*, vol. 6, p. 166)

> Sound an alarm throughout the length and breadth of the land. Tell the people that the day of the Lord is near, and hasteth greatly. Let none be left unwarned. Having heard the solemn warning of the third angel, we are debtors to others, to impart the truth to them. ("A Call to Service," *The Watchman*, June 18, 1907)

> Who are voicing the message of the third angel, telling the world to make ready for the great day of God? The message we bear to the world has the seal of the living God. The Scriptures of the Old and New Testaments are to be combined in

the work of fitting up a people to stand in the day of the Lord. (*Manuscript Releases*, vol. 13, p. 268)

In the next section we will apply the truths of the third angel's message to the book of Joel.

The Third Angel's Message and the Book of Joel

The book of Joel in the Old Testament warns against the day of the Lord. Joel, whose name means "Yahweh is God," was one of twelve minor prophets. The book is three chapters in length, and it mentions the day of the Lord in five verses (Joel 1:15; 2:1, 11, 31; 3:14). After a brief introduction, the prophet presents this question: "Hear this, ye old men, and give ear, all ye inhabitants of the land. Hath this been in your days, or even in the days of your fathers?" (Joel 1:2).

With such an abrupt and fearful beginning, the following questions may be asked. What message were the people to "hear" and "give ear" to? What event is the verse referring to? What event had not been in "their day" or "the day of their fathers"? After reading chapter one the following conclusions may be drawn:

- He talks about a coming unprecedented calamity, an event that was unheard of by the fathers (Joel 1:2).

- He talks about devastation by a plague of locusts (Joel 1:4).
- He talks about a coming judgment that would be unparalleled in intensity and totality (Joel 1:4).

In Joel 1:2 the prophet addresses the "old men" and all the inhabitants of the land. He re-addresses his audience in verses 14 and 15: "Sanctify ye a fast, call a solemn assembly, gather the elders and all the inhabitants of the land into the house of the LORD your God, and cry unto the LORD, Alas for the day! for the day of the LORD is at hand, and as a destruction from the Almighty shall it come." We may further conclude that Joel's message is a warning against the day of the Lord (Joel 1:15).

The prophet's message to Zion, God's holy mountain, and "all the inhabitants of the land" continues in Joel 2:1. "Blow ye the trumpet in Zion, and sound an alarm in my holy mountain: let all the inhabitants of the land tremble: for the day of the LORD cometh, for it is nigh at hand."

After reading this verse the following assessments may be made:

- Joel's message is a warning message and an alarming message.
- This message is for all the inhabitants of the land.

- It is a warning that the day of the Lord approaches.

The language used by the prophet to describe the destroying locusts has striking similarities to that used in Exodus 10:6: "And they shall fill thy houses, and the houses of all thy servants, and the houses of all the Egyptians; which neither thy fathers, nor thy fathers' fathers have seen, since the day that they were upon the earth unto this day." The plague of locusts that Joel described for his day was to be of such severity that he borrowed the language used by Moses when characterizing the plague in Egypt.

Joel's fearful warning was addressed to Zion, and God's holy mountain, which is a reference for God's people. We read the following in Micah 4:1, 2: "But in the last days it shall come to pass, that the mountain of the house of the LORD shall be established in the top of the mountains, and it shall be exalted above the hills; and people shall flow unto it. And many nations shall come, and say, Come, and let us go up to the mountain of the LORD, and to the house of the God of Jacob; and he will teach us of his ways, and we will walk in his paths: for the law shall go forth of Zion, and the word of the LORD from Jerusalem."

The holy mountain as mentioned by Zechariah is a reference to God's people. "Thus saith the LORD; I am returned unto Zion, and will dwell in the midst of

Jerusalem: and Jerusalem shall be called a city of truth; and the mountain of the Lord of hosts the holy mountain" (Zech. 8:3). "Zion" and "My holy mountain" also signify God's present day church. The apostle Paul writes, that "all these things happened unto them for ensamples: and they are written for our admonition, upon whom the ends of the world are come" (1 Cor. 10:11). Ellen White wrote the following, "The prophets spoke less for their own time than for the ages which have followed, and for our own day" ("Heart Piety Essential," *The Signs of the Times,* April 2, 1896). "All the inhabitants of the land" not only refers to God's people in the entire world, but to all mankind as the day of the Lord will involve all the inhabitants of the earth.

> *The third angel's message is to be at this time regarded as of the highest importance. It is a life-and-death question.*

Integrating the truths that we have covered, we ask the following question: When did Joel 1:2 speak "for our own day?" Alternatively, we may ask, what message for our day refers to an event unheard of by the "fathers," warns against the day of the Lord, makes reference to plagues, warns of a coming judgment that will be unparalleled in intensity and totality, warns of an unprecedented calamity, and addresses all the inhabitants of the land? To which message are we to blow a trumpet and sound an alarm, to hear and give ear to?

The following quotes from the Spirit of Prophecy provide us with insight into these questions:

> We know that now everything is at stake. The third angel's message is to be at this time regarded as of the highest importance. It is a life-and-death question. (*Manuscript Releases*, vol. 9, p. 290)

> The third angel's message in its clear, definite terms is to be made the prominent warning. (*Manuscript Releases*, vol. 2, p. 19)

> A parchment was placed in the angel's hand, and as he descended to the earth in power and majesty, he proclaimed a fearful warning, with the most terrible threatening ever borne to man. (*Early Writings*, p. 254)

> The theme of greatest importance is the third angel's message, embracing the messages

The Third Angel's Message and the Book of Joel

of the first and second angels (*Evangelism*,
p. 196)

The third angel's message is the Gospel
message for these last days. (*The Kress
Collection*, p. 102)

Consider the similarities between the following quote
from the Spirit of Prophecy and Joel 2:1: "Sound an alarm
throughout the length and breadth of the land. Tell the
people that the day of the
Lord is near, and hasteth
greatly. Let none be left
unwarned. Having heard the
solemn warning of the third
angel, we are debtors to others, to impart the truth to
them" ("A Call to Service,"
The Watchman, June 18,
1907). Joel 2:1 reads, "Blow ye the trumpet in Zion, and
sound an alarm in my holy mountain: let all the inhabitants of the land tremble: for the day of the LORD cometh,
for it is nigh at hand."

> *It wasn't until the "sealing message" was established that the truths of the third angel's message were well understood.*

Upon comparing the statements, it is evident that Ellen
White associated the third angel's message with the message

of Joel. In 1848 the clear light regarding the "sealing truth" was given to Ellen White. She said, "At a meeting held in Dorchester, Mass., November, 1848, I had been given a view of the proclamation of the sealing message, and of the duty of the brethren to publish the light that was shining upon our pathway" (*Life Sketches of Ellen G. White*, p. 125). It wasn't until the "sealing message" was established that the truths of the third angel's message were well understood. In 1848 the truths of the third angel's message were "very well defined, and the way was opening in different directions for the advancement of the work" (Loughborough, *The Great Second Advent Movement: Its Rise and Progress*, p. 149).

To summarize, the third angel's message and Joel's message share many comparable themes. These similarities include reference to events unheard of by the "fathers"; warning against the day of the Lord; making reference to plagues; warning of a coming judgment that would be unparalleled in intensity and totality; warning of an unprecedented calamity; and addressing all the inhabitants of the land. We are to blow a trumpet and sound an alarm for both messages as they are messages that we are to hear and give ear to.

In conclusion, Joel 1:2 spoke "for our own day," became present truth, and was fulfilled in 1848 with the commencement of the third angel's message.

The First Publishing Ventures

Let's now turn our attention to Joel 1:3: "Tell ye your children of it, and let your children tell their children, and their children another generation."

When did the first portion of the verse regarding "tell ye" become present truth? What starting date can we give it? In the book *The Publishing Ministry*, chapter one, we read about the Dorchester Vision of 1848 and the "first publishing ventures." It was in Dorchester, Massachusetts, that Ellen White received a vision of the "sealing message," which clearly defined the third angel's message. We established that "the third angel's message is the Gospel message for these last days" (White, *The Kress Collection*, p. 102).

In September of 1848 James and Ellen White journeyed to Maine to attend the Topsham conference. They gathered with the believers and prayed that a way might be opened to publish the truths connected with the advent message. A month later they were assembled with a small company, along with Joseph Bates, in Dorchester,

Massachusetts. The small group made the publication of "the sealing message" a subject of prayer. Disputes arose among them as to what was the sealing. They resolved to refer it all to God. After some time in earnest prayer for light and instruction, God gave Ellen White a vision.

James White wrote the following about the meeting: "We all felt like uniting to ask wisdom from God on the points in dispute; also Brother Bates's duty in writing. We had an exceedingly powerful meeting. Ellen was again taken off in vision. She then began to describe the Sabbath light, which was the sealing truth" (White, *Life Sketches of Ellen G. White*, p. 116).

It was after this vision that Mrs. White informed her husband of his duty to publish, and that as he should advance by faith, success would attend his efforts. Regarding this vision of November 18, 1848, Elder Joseph Bates testified that he saw and heard the following from the lips of Ellen Harmon: " 'Yea, publish the things thou hast seen and heard, and the blessing of God will attend.' ... At a meeting held in Dorchester, Mass., November, 1848, I had been given a view of the proclamation of the sealing message, and of the duty of the brethren to publish the light that was shining upon our pathway" (White, *The Publishing Ministry*, p. 15). The first article was written and published in Middletown,

Connecticut in July of the following year and was titled "The Present Truth."

We have established that in 1848 the spreading of the great truths connected with the third angel's message began (Emmerson, *The Reformation and the Advent Movement,* p. 206). That year the truths of the third angel's message were "very well defined and the way was opening in different directions for the advancement of the work" (Loughborough, *The Great Second Advent Movement: Its Rise and Progress*, p. 149).

The phrase "tell ye" at the beginning of Joel 1:3 refers to the "first publishing venture" that started in 1848; the same year the sealing message identified the Sabbath as the seal of God, which helped to fully define the third angel's message. "The third angel's message is the Gospel message for these last days" (White, *The Kress Collection*, p. 102). To reiterate, we have established that Joel 1:2 is for our day and signaled the commencement of the proclamation of the third angel's message in 1848.

The Four Generations

Now we will take a look at the latter part of Joel 1:3 that mentions four generations: "Tell ye your children of it, and let your children tell their children, and their children another generation." The four generations here are believed to be referring to God's people at the end of the world and the four generations their prophetic history. What is the prophetic significance of the time period represented here?

The prophet Joel declares that we may know when the day of the Lord is at hand (Joel 1:15; 2:1). The pioneers understood and believed this to be the case. Brother Loughborough wrote, "God, by Joel, commanded, when the great day of God should be at hand" (*The Great Second Advent Movement: Its Rise and Progress*, p. 90). Ellen White, in describing the 1844 movement, stated, "As God by Joel commanded, when the great day of God should be at hand, it produced a rending of hearts and not of garments, and a turning unto the Lord with fasting, and weeping, and mourning" (*The Great Controversy*, p. 401). What does it mean for the day of the Lord to be at hand? To answer this question, we turn to Luke 21:31, 32: "So likewise ye, when ye see these things come to pass, know ye that the kingdom of God is nigh at hand. Verily I say unto you, this generation shall not pass away, till all be fulfilled."

When Luke wrote "these things," he was referring to the signs that were to precede the second coming of Jesus. The last of the signs to be fulfilled was "distress of nations, with perplexity" (Luke 21:25). It is clear that Ellen White believed that those who witnessed this sign should not pass away until Christ returned. "Since that time earthquakes, tempests, tidal waves, pestilence, famine, and destructions by fire and flood, have multiplied. All these, and 'distress of nations, with perplexity,' declare that the Lord's coming is near. Of those who beheld these signs He says, 'This generation shall not pass, till all these things be fulfilled'" (*The Story of Jesus*, p. 176). The Bible, in no uncertain terms, has given us clear and distinct rays of light revealing that the day of the Lord is near at the doors (White, *Counsels for the Church,* p. 64). At what point in history was this sign fulfilled? We have been instructed that the fulfillment of prophetic events has been recorded on the pages of history (White, *Prophets and Kings*, p. 536). The signs of the sun, moon and stars were all specific events which have been documented on the pages of history. The last of these signs was fulfilled in the days of the pioneers in the year 1833. Therefore, what specific event would fulfill the last sign given; the "distress of nations, with perplexity"?

The key to figuring out the fulfillment of this event is to search out the original meaning of the word "perplexity." The original word that is used in the Greek is *aporia*, which is defined as:

1. Of places, difficulty of passing
    a. Of things, difficulty, straits, impasse, no way out
    b. Of persons, difficulty of dealing with
2. Lack of wealth, means or resources, embarrassment, difficulty, hesitation, perplexity
3. Want of a person or thing
4. Absolute poverty

The use of the word *aporia* in the verse conveys the idea of the inability of the nations to meet financial demands. The question we now ask is: When has there been distress of nations upon this earth with no way out of the dire straits ahead and a lack of resources, which leads to poverty? I believe that the last sign to precede Christ's return, which is mentioned in Luke 21:25—"distress of nations, with perplexity"—was fulfilled in the great global recession of 2008. It was this year that the kingdom of God was "nigh at hand" (Luke 21:31) or "nigh, even at the doors" (Mark 13:29). Jesus then declares, "Verily I say unto you, that this generation shall not pass, till all these things be done" (Mark 13:30).

Now that we have established a definition and year for the term "nigh at hand," let us look at the prophetic significance of the four generations of Joel 1:3. God commanded the prophet Joel when the great day of the Lord should be at hand. We have established that 1848 was the starting time of the spreading of the third angel's message through the first publishing venture. If a biblical generation is forty years, as indicated in Numbers 32:13, we may conclude that Joel's prophecy extends 160 years from 1848. It is evident to see that the prophet Joel declares that the day of the Lord became 'nigh at hand' in 2008, which is in agreement with the prophetic sign given in the book of Luke about the distress of nations, with perplexity. It is from this point that Jesus declares, "Verily I say unto you, that this generation shall not pass away, till all these things be done."

In the Mouth of Two or Three Witnesses

The apostle Paul wrote, "In the mouth of two or three witnesses shall every word be established" (2 Cor. 13:1). Are there other writers of Holy Scripture besides Joel and Luke who mention that the coming of the Lord is near? James declared: "Be ye also patient; stablish your hearts: for the coming of the Lord draweth nigh. Grudge not one against another, brethren, lest ye be condemned: behold, the judge standeth before the door" (James 5:8, 9).

A few verses earlier, James wrote, "Ye have lived in pleasure on the earth, and been wanton; ye have nourished your hearts, as in a day of slaughter" (verse 5). The day of slaughter referred to here is synonymous with a "day of judgment." It is one of the many biblical references to the day of the Lord. The prophet Isaiah, in foretelling of the destruction of spiritual Babylon, wrote, "And there shall be upon every high mountain, and upon every high hill, rivers and streams of waters in the day of the great slaughter, when the towers fall" (Isa. 30:25). Furthermore, James prophesied of the last days, declaring, "Your gold

and silver is cankered; and the rust of them shall be a witness against you, and shall eat your flesh as it were fire. Ye
have heaped treasure together for the last days" (James
5:3). It is evident that James chapter 5 is relevant for its
present truth.

What event does James write about to indicate that the
Lord's coming is near? Ellen White wrote the following,
"The Scriptures describe the condition of the world just
before Christ's second coming. The apostle James pictures
the greed and oppression that will prevail" ("Nearness of
the End," *The Review and Herald,* March 14, 1912).

Gretchen Morgenson, a business reporter for the *New
York Times*, co-authored a book about the origin of the
2008 financial meltdown. In *Reckless Endangerment: How
Outsized Ambition, Greed and Corruption Led to Economic
Armageddon*, she describes how regulators failed to con-
trol greed and recklessness on Wall Street. She relates
how companies manipulated accounting rules, generated
large salaries and bonuses for executives, used lobby and
campaign contributions to bully regulators, and undertook
risky financial practices that led to the crisis.

The apostle James saw that greed and oppression
would reach a climax in the days preceding the coming
of the Lord (*The SDA Bible Commentary*, vol. 7, p. 537).
We conclude that James 5:8, 9 met its fulfillment when the

greed and oppression that the apostle condemned reached a climax in 2008 and led to or "set off" the global recession that Ellen White predicted would occur just before Christ's second coming.

Turning back to the Old Testament, we read about Zephaniah's ministry in the seventh century BC during the reign of Josiah, king of Judah. This prophet of God also warned when the day of the Lord would be at hand (Zeph. 1:7). Among the sins that called down the judgments of God were the greed and corruption that were prevalent in Jerusalem. "And it shall come to pass in that day, saith the LORD, that there shall be the noise of a cry from the fish gate, and an howling from the second, and a great crashing from the hills. Howl, ye inhabitants of Maktesh, for all the merchant people are cut down; all they that bear silver are cut off" (Zeph. 1:10, 11).

The fish gate was one of the main centers of commerce in the city of Jerusalem. It was a place of various economic activities. The merchants not only sold fish, but also various types of wares, which refers to different articles of merchandise (Neh. 13:16, 20). It was a place where merchants and usurers added to their wealth through dishonest trade and lending money at unreasonably high rates of interest. The fish gate was specifically mentioned by the prophet as a place that was to be visited by God's judgments.

Zephaniah mentioned Maktesh in his prophecy, which was a street in Jerusalem distinguished for its commerce and is conceivably a representation of modern-day Wall Street. Its merchants would have had reason to mourn when the city was made desolate. Covetousness and corruption were the order of the day as the inhabitants added to their ill-gotten gains. The prophet further admonished them that "neither their silver nor their gold shall be able to deliver them in the day of the LORD's wrath" (Zeph. 1:18).

The great day of the Lord as prophesied by Zephaniah met a partial fulfillment in his day when Jerusalem was destroyed by Babylon, but the final great day of the Lord is to come when the world will be destroyed. The fish gate and the street of Maktesh were commercial districts that were singled out by the prophet to receive the retributive judgments of God. These two centers of trade serve as types of the modern day economic greed and corruption that reached its climax in the global financial crisis of 2008. As Zephaniah declared for our day, the day of the Lord is at hand.

Conclusion

Various authors of Scripture have prophesied for our day foretelling when the great day of the Lord would be at hand. "All these things happened unto them for ensamples: and they are written for our admonition, upon whom the ends of the world are come" (1 Cor. 10:11). The books of Joel, Luke, James, and Zephaniah have given us prophetic signs that we may know when His coming is near at hand. They have spoken more for our present day and for the generations that have followed them than for the times in which they lived.

The great global recession of 2008 was a prophetic event that indicated that Jesus arrived "at the door" and that this present generation will not pass until He shall return in the clouds of heaven. Jesus said, "So ye in like manner, when ye shall see these things come to pass, know that it is nigh, even at the doors. Verily I say unto you, that this generation shall not pass, till all these things be done" (Mark 13:29, 30).

"Watch ye therefore: for ye know not when the master of the house cometh, at even, or at midnight, or at the cockcrowing, or in the morning" (Mark 13:35). The hours of a typical watch are divided into four periods: the evening watch, 6:00 p.m. to 9:00 p.m.; the midnight hour, 9:00 p.m. to 12:00 a.m.; the cockcrowing, 12:00 a.m. to 3:00 a.m.;

and the morning watch, 3:00 a.m. to 6:00 a.m. Therefore, I feel that we may divide the last generation (a biblical generation being forty years) as follows: at even, 2008–2018; at midnight, 2018–2028; at the cockcrowing, 2028–2038; or in the morning, 2038–2048. Although prophecy does not reveal the day or the hour of His coming, so near an approximation has been given that we may know when we have come to the generation that will not pass before Christ returns in the clouds of glory.

The apostle Paul wrote that God "will finish the work, and cut it short in righteousness: because a short work will the Lord make upon the earth" (Rom. 9:28). "And that, knowing the time, that now it is high time to awake out of sleep: for now is our salvation nearer than when we believed" (Rom. 13:11). God's sleeping children of Laodicea would do well to anoint their eyes with eyesalve that they may discern the signs of the times (Rev. 3:18). To be as "the children of Issachar, which were men that had understanding of the times, to know what Israel ought to do" (1 Chron. 12:32).

Joel declared, "Blow ye the trumpet in Zion, and sound an alarm in my holy mountain: let all the inhabitants of the land tremble: for the day of the LORD cometh, for it is nigh at hand" (Joel 2:1). The watchmen on the walls of Zion need to sound an alarm throughout the length and breadth of the land, declaring to the people that the great day of the Lord is near at hand (Zeph. 1:14). Having the light of the third angel's message, we are obligated to impart the truth to others. May we do our duty in warning the world of Christ's soon coming.

We conclude with the words of Joel:

> Therefore also now, saith the LORD, turn ye even to me with all your heart, and with fasting, and with weeping, and with mourning: and rend your heart, and not your garments, and turn unto the LORD your God: for he is gracious and merciful, slow to anger, and of great kindness, and repenteth him of the evil. Who knoweth if he will return and repent, and leave a blessing behind him; even a meat offering and a drink offering unto the LORD your God? Blow the trumpet in Zion, sanctify a fast, call a solemn assembly. Gather the people, sanctify the congregation, assemble the elders, gather the children, and those that suck the breasts: let the bridegroom go forth of his chamber, and the bride out of her closet. Let the priests, the ministers of

the LORD, weep between the porch and the altar, and let them say, Spare thy people, O LORD, and give not thine heritage to reproach. (Joel 2:12–17)

Bibliography

Emmerson, W. L. *The Reformation and the Advent Movement*. Hagerstown, MD: Review and Herald Publishing Association, 1983.

Loughborough, J. N. *The Great Second Advent Movement: Its Rise and Progress.* Ringgold, GA: TEACH Services Inc., 2013.

Morgenson, Gretchen, and Joshua Rosner. *Reckless Endangerment: How Outsized Ambition, Greed, and Corruption Led to Economic Armageddon.* New York, NY: Times Books, 2011.

The SDA Bible Commentary. Vol. 7. Washington, DC: Review and Herald Publishing Association, 1957.

Smith, Uriah. *Daniel and the Revelation.* Battle Creek, MI: Review and Herald Publishing Association, 1897.

White, Ellen G. "A Call to Service." *The Watchman,* June 18, 1907.

———. *Christ Triumphant.* Hagerstown, MD: Review and Herald Publishing Association, 1999.

———. *Counsels for the Church.* Nampa, ID: Pacific Press Publishing Association, 1991.

———. *Early Writings.* Washington, DC: Review and Herald Publishing Association, 1882.

———. *Evangelism.* Washington, DC: Review and Herald Publishing Association, 1946.

———. *The Great Controversy.* Mountain View, CA: Pacific Press Publishing Association, 1911.

———. "Heart Piety Essential." *The Signs of the Times,* April 2, 1896.

———. *The Kress Collection.* Payson, AZ: Leaves-of-Autumn Books, 1985.

———. *Life Sketches of Ellen G. White.* Mountain View, CA: Pacific Press Publishing Association, 1915.

———. *Manuscript Releases.* Vol. 1. Silver Spring, MD: Ellen G. White Estate, 1981.

———. *Manuscript Releases.* Vol. 2. Silver Spring, MD: Ellen G. White Estate, 1987.

———. *Manuscript Releases.* Vol. 9. Silver Spring, MD: Ellen G. White Estate, 1990.

———. *Manuscript Releases.* Vol. 13. Silver Spring, MD: Ellen G. White Estate, 1987.

———. *Manuscript Releases.* Vol. 19. Silver Spring, MD: Ellen G. White Estate, 1990.

———. "Nearness of the End." *The Review and Herald,* March 14, 1912.

———. *Prophets and Kings.* Mountain View, CA: Pacific Press Publishing Association, 1917.

————. *The Publishing Ministry.* Hagerstown, MD: Review and Herald Publishing Association, 1983.

————. *Testimonies for the Church.* Vol. 6. Mountain View, CA: Pacific Press Publishing Association, 1901.

————. *A Word to the Little Flock.* Washington, DC: Review and Herald Publishing Association, 1847.

We invite you to view the complete
selection of titles we publish at:

www.AspectBooks.com

Scan with your mobile
device to go directly
to our website.

Please write or email us your praises, reactions, or
thoughts about this or any other book we publish at:

AB ASPECT Books
www.ASPECTBooks.com

P.O. Box 954
Ringgold, GA 30736

info@AspectBooks.com

Aspect Books titles may be purchased in bulk for
educational, business, fund-raising, or sales promotional use.
For information, please e-mail

BulkSales@AspectBooks.com

Finally, if you are interested in seeing
your own book in print, please contact us at

publishing@AspectBooks.com

We would be happy to review your manuscript for free.

www.ingramcontent.com/pod-product-compliance
Lightning Source LLC
Chambersburg PA
CBHW071751090426
42738CB00011B/2648